GRIEF IN YOUR WORDS

How Writing Helps You Heal

HARRIET HODGSON

North Carolina

Published in the United States by WriteLife Publishing
(an imprint of Boutique of Quality Books Publishing Company, Inc.)
www.writelife.com

978-1-60808-297-1 (p)
978-1-60808-298-8 (e)

Library of Congress Control Number: 2024931292

Book design by Robin Krauss, www.bookformatters.com
Cover design by Rebecca Lown, www.rebeccalowndesign.com

First Editor: Andrea Vande Vorde
Second Editor: Allison Itterly

Praise for Harriet Hodgson and Grief in Your Words

"We rationally know that death is a part of the human experience; nevertheless, when we lose a loved one to death, rationality takes a back seat to unrelenting grief. Ms. Hodgson's *Grief in Your Words* supplies a welcome avenue for healing through expressing our thoughts via the written word.

Her powerful yet sensitive statements about grief, accompanied by practical exercises, lead the reader toward a better understanding of the process of grieving and offer guidance and words of comfort through difficult states when any sense of control might seem distant. An important book."

Bonnie Johnson, PhD, Professor, Department of Education Specialties, St. John's University, New York City

---

"Grief doesn't only come with death; it can come with any loss, including the loss of a relationship, loss of a career, loss of a way of life, or the loss of a dream. Writing down your thoughts and feelings is a practical way to process all the emotions attached to loss and the grief that follows.

Harriet Hodgson's book, *Grief in Your Words: How Writing Helps You Heal*, will help you process loss, or change and track your reflections, experiences, and feelings over time. The thoughtful prompts will guide you as you begin your journey to healing.

In a time when so many of us are facing loss, *Grief in Your Words: How Writing Helps You Heal*, is an easy-to-follow, comforting companion through the many aspects of grief. Full of practical and engaging activities, evidence-based suggestions, and inspiring words of wisdom, this book is like having a trusted friend, therapist, and a grief guide by your side at all times."

Gary Sturgis, Grief Specialist, Grief Speaker, Bereavement Facilitator,
bestselling author of *Surviving Grief—365 Days a Year*

"Although I am familiar with art therapy as a way of dealing with grief, Harriet Hodgson provides yet another excellent creative resource for exploring the different ways humans respond to the death of their loved ones in *Grief in Your Words: How Writing Helps You Heal*. This practical handbook providers readers with specific steps to assist them in making sense of the many, sometimes nebulous emotions we all experience when someone close to us dies.

Using her own deep familiarity with loss, Hodgson provides specific questions to assist us in putting our feelings down on paper as a way of moving through the grieving process. Along with reassurance that this process may one day become manageable, she gives suggestions for such situations as dealing with anniversary reactions, responding to the well-meaning but answerless question, 'How are you?' and developing methods of self-care.

An excellent bibliography of support resources accompanies the text. *Grief in Your Words* is an easy, helpful read."

Kenneth Counselman, PhD, retired Professor,
Wheelock College of Education and Human Development

"*Grief in Your Words* offers a step-by-step approach to process your thoughts and feelings associated with grief. The book is full of practical insights and has meaningful prompts to help even a reluctant writer. This book would be a wonderful resource for grief groups or even a family looking to better understand how each one is coping. Knowing Harriet Hodgson, I can hear her gentle voice encouraging the reader with humor and practicality. As a grief counselor, this book is on my resource list as a valuable tool for those who are trying to make sense of their grief journey. Thank you once again Harriet!"

Heidi Smith, Licensed Professional Counselor, LPCC, Thanatology Fellow

"*Grief in Your Words* is like a warm hug from a friend. There is so much wisdom, encouragement, resources, and support wrapped up in the power of writing as a powerful tool to help and support every aspect of a grief journey. The book explores how simple, easy, and insightful writing can be and makes it as simple as possible with writing prompts, one-word writing and more. This book is easy to use with step-by-step instructions. It would be wonderful to use in a support group setting for older adults—a book you will turn to again and again."

Kathy Scheid, Executive Director, Elder Network, Rochester, Minnesota

"When you're experiencing the loss of a loved one, it may seem that there is no way to go on. Harriet Hodgson knows this from first-hand experience, and in her remarkable new book, provides a guide to navigating loss.

Besides making suggestions on making it through the fog of grief, the author offers practical advice on adding meaning to every day. This includes things like finding ways to share your loved one's values, dealing with the question, 'How are you?' and coping with the pain that comes with holidays.

One of the strategies she highlights is putting words down on paper. Writing your grief story helps you heal, she observes, and *Grief in Your Words* shows you how. Written with compassion and empathy, this is a book you will want to share with others when the hard times come."

Lucy Adkins, author of *Two-Toned Dress* and *A Crazy Little Things*,
co-author of *Writing in Community* and *The Fire Inside*

"Grief escapes no one, but Harriet Hodgson writes from a position of experience and multiple tragic circumstances. A survivor and ultimate thriver, she skillfully describes her grief journey. The purpose of her book is to encourage the reader to express their grief in words. Harriet's gentle approach and writing prompts will give the reader the impetus to begin this healing practice."

Lois Ruth Kennel, retired English teacher

This book is dedicated to all who grieve,
and work so hard to heal.

CONTENTS

Making the Most of This Book   xi

Preface   xvii

Part 1: Getting Ready to Write   1

Chapter 1: The Benefits of Writing   3

Chapter 2: Choosing the Best Writing Form for You   7

Chapter 3: Gathering Your Materials   11

Chapter 4: Finding a Place to Write   13

Chapter 5: The Joy of Journal Writing   17

Chapter 6: Brainstorming about Writing Ideas   21

Part 2: Readings to Jump-Start Writing   27

Chapter 7: Coping with Grief: Your Mental Toolkit   29

Chapter 8: Receiving the Gift of Food   33

Chapter 9: Setting Goals After a Loved One Dies   37

Chapter 10: Living a Loved One's Values   41

Chapter 11: The Miracles of Kindness   45

Chapter 12: Time is Different When You're Grieving   49

Chapter 13: The Benefits of Exercise   53

Chapter 14: Having a Relationship with the Deceased   57

Chapter 15: Honor a Loved One with Their Favorite Dinner   61

Chapter 16: Got Grief Brain?   65

Chapter 17: When Does the Crying Stop?   69

Chapter 18: Coping with Anniversary Reactions   73

Chapter 19: Answering the Question "How are You?"   77

Chapter 20: Creating a Memory Cookbook   81

Chapter 21: Giving Yourself Permission to Laugh   85

Chapter 22: Be Grateful for Writing   89

Part 3: Finishing the Job   **93**

Chapter 23: Reviewing Your Words   95

Chapter 24: Writing and Personal Growth   97

Chapter 25: Self-Care Steps   101

Chapter 26: Words of Hope   109

Conclusion: A Good Ending to a Grief Story   **113**

Other Journal Ideas to Explore   **117**

Journal Pages   **119**

Support for You   **133**

Bibliography   **137**

More Grief Healing Books by Harriet Hodgson   **141**

About the Author   **143**

Making the Most of This Book

You must remember that your story matters.
What you write has the power to save a life, [and] sometimes that life is your own.
— Stalina Goodwin

You are worthy of self-care. *Grief in Your Words* is a form of self-care. This book provides spaces for you to write to help guide you through the grief maze, allowing you to emerge from it and live the new life that's waiting for you. To do this, you need to tell your grief story—a story that is as unique as you are.

Your story is yours alone, an agonizing, confusing, stressful story. You may feel like you've lost control over life. And maybe you have. But a lack of control is temporary and can be regained. This book is your personal writing plan, one designed just for you. The writing plan has six steps that move from ideas to action. As your words accumulate, you may see a glimmer of hope. Having a writing plan can give you hope too.

Writing Plan

1. A willingness to express your thoughts in words.
2. Finding a comfortable writing place.
3. Brainstorming about writing topics.
4. Putting words on paper.

5. Evaluating your writing.
6. Applying what you learn from writing to your life.

The sixth step may be the most important. Expressing your grief story with words helps only if you learn from the process.

Many positive things can result from writing. For example, when you write about grief, it may help you realize you're trying to pack too much into a day. Consequently, you simplify your days and feel less stressed. Writing also helps you identify problems, such as not having a legal will, and for you to rectify this problem.

Having the determination to write doesn't mean you're going to produce a best-selling novel, although that would be fabulous. Instead, it means you review your story, divide it into parts, engage in introspection, and document your story in words. The purpose of this book is simple: to encourage you to write. What you write depends on your feelings and grief experience.

The idea of writing may make you nervous. Well, you can relax. I won't toss you off the dock into the writing sea. *Grief in Your Words* eases you into writing and lets you proceed at your own pace. Better yet, you are always in control. You decide the topics to write about, when you write, what you write, and how much you write.

Each chapter begins with an inspiring quote. I love all the quotes—after all, I chose them—but I have a favorite. Flannery O'Connor, an American novelist, short story writer, and essayist, eloquently says: "I write because I don't know what I think until I read what I say."

What a profound sentence. This sentence resonated with me because I've lived it and literally wrote my way to healing. The more I wrote, the more I understood my grief journey. When I look back at my life, I can barely believe I survived. This may be true for you too. Seeing thoughts on paper can help you identify what you want to say and need to say for healing to happen.

As you write, you may begin to realize you aren't merely surviving: you are thriving and preparing for the future. Writing helps you learn about yourself, unveiling aspects that you may not have known before, and offer insights about the grief process in general.

Part 1, "Getting Ready to Write," focuses on preparation and gathering supplies. Just as you gather ingredients for a recipe, you gather writing supplies and keep them close at hand. Having extra packs of printer paper is an example of gathering supplies.

Part 2, "Readings to Jump-Start Writing," contains articles on a variety of topics, including traumatic loss, "grief brain" (a common response to the death of a loved one), setting goals, accepting acts of kindness, staying physically active, and coping with anniversary reactions (i.e., a particular day of the year in which feelings of grief resurface). At the end of each article, there is a writing prompt and a lined page where you can jot down your thoughts.

I would suggest dating your writing for reference. Having a date helps you and future generations to understand family history, the challenges you faced, and how you coped with them. Instead of giving up, you stood up for yourself and were proactive.

Part 3, "Finishing the Job," focuses on reviewing your writing, the topics you write about, your word choices, and what you have learned from expressing your grief. Evaluating your writing can be a slow process, one that could take weeks or months. Hidden thoughts may suddenly emerge. Established thoughts may become stronger. Be patient and give yourself the gift of time.

Complete the writing exercises when you're ready. Relatives and well-meaning friends may think you'll recover from grief in a few weeks. Don't believe this myth or succumb to pressure. Be kind to yourself during this trying time of life and set your own pace. Take a break if you feel tired. Reread a section if you feel it's necessary. Set the book aside for a few days and continue reading later. *Grief in Your Words* is a springboard to healing and may be used in several ways.

Share *Grief in Your Words* with your faith community.

You may decide to share *Grief in Your Words* in faith-based groups such as Sunday School or discussions after church. Each person in the group has their own copy of the book and contributes to the discussion. Writing and speaking about grief is a learning process. Everyone should have the opportunity to speak at a group meeting. You may hear stories that are similar to yours and discover possible solutions to your problems.

Use *Grief in Your Words* as a workshop resource.

You may take a workshop that talks about grief: the physical and emotional effects, coping ideas, sources of support, and planning a new life. Again, each member of the group has their own copy of the book. Grief is far-reaching, and class discussions can also be far-reaching. Remember, you don't have to agree with every point to benefit from the discussion.

Discuss *Grief in Your Words* in a reading group.

If you belong to a book club, suggest *Grief in Your Words* as the book of the week or month. If you don't belong to one, consider starting your own reading group. The group doesn't have to be large. Even three people can gather regularly to discuss the books they've read. You may also find a reading buddy, and the two of you may discuss the book together.

Use *Grief in Your Words* in support group meetings.

The group facilitator should be a qualified person: someone with a degree in counseling or social work, someone who has led groups before, or someone who is considered an expert due to their extensive grief experience. The facilitator directs the group. With the facilitator's help, group members determine the ebb and flow of the discussion. Confidentiality is paramount, and you follow the rule: "What we say here is just between us." The writing steps and topic ideas in this book may spark group discussions. For example, you may have a discussion with another group member about the benefits of grief journaling during the grieving process.

Give away copies of *Grief in Your Words.*

Give this book to a grieving relative or friend. Donate a copy to your local public library or to your religious community library. You can intentionally leave a copy in a public place, such as the airport, with the hope that it will help another person who is grieving. Sharing is a proactive step and makes you feel good inside.

Allow *Grief in Your Words* to lead you to healing.

Though you have the same symptoms as others who are grieving, you cope in your own way and time. As the months pass, you come to realize that grief has valuable lessons that you can grow from. This growth may be painful and satisfying at the same time. Yet it's still growth and signifies that you're moving forward on the healing path.

Grief in Your Words can be a buddy, a ray of light that brightens your way. Please make it your own. Underline points, write notes in the margins, fold down page corners, and put sticky notes on pages you want to read again. The death of a loved one is life's greatest pain. I can't take away your pain, but I can offer words of comfort.

There is hope. This is your book, your story, and your healing path. I wish you safe travels on the journey.

Preface

Writing songs is my therapy. It helps me make sense of my feelings.
— **Ed Sheeran**

You never know what life will send your way. That may be a good thing. If you knew the future, you would worry and grieve too early. On February 23, 2007, I had no inkling of the grief that awaited me. That day, my oldest daughter, Helen, tragically lost her life in a car accident. Surgeons operated on her for twenty hours in a desperate attempt to save her life, but my daughter's injuries were so severe that their attempts were to no avail. Still, I am grateful for their efforts and expertise.

My twin grandchildren, who were fifteen years old at the time, went into shock at their mother's death, especially my granddaughter. She was in the car during the accident and suffered a mild concussion. After an overnight stay in the hospital, she was discharged. These circumstances forced my husband, John, and me to make painful decisions and make them quickly.

We contacted the funeral home, chose a casket, purchased a burial plot, reserved a date for the church memorial service, helped plan the service, found a photo for the program, edited the program, chose photos for a slide presentation, and sent an obituary to the newspaper. Amazingly, we accomplished all of this in two days, and I was proud of us. Even in the face of traumatic loss, my husband and I worked as a team.

But the burial and memorial arrangements were so agonizing that I wanted to go to bed, hide under a blanket, curl up in the fetal position, and sob for days.

My former son-in-law, whom Helen had divorced about three years earlier, offered to move into the house Helen bought for the twins and live there until they graduated from high school. We accepted his offer. The twins had enough changes to deal with and didn't need any more. Staying in their home in the same neighborhood, surrounded by familiar things, including their dog, would comfort them.

While I grieved for my daughter, I anticipated my father-in-law's death. Dad had pneumonia and coughed so much the assisted living staff sent him to the hospital by ambulance. After a week's stay, doctors realized they couldn't save Dad's life. He was just too frail, and being a retired physician, he knew it. He asked for no special measures to be taken and returned to his assisted living apartment, and a few days later, he died. He was just six months shy of his ninety-ninth birthday.

Unlike my daughter's sudden death, I had anticipated Dad's death and was somewhat prepared for it. Dad had lived a long, productive, and happy life. Yet it was heart-wrenching to see his obituary and my daughter's obituary on the same page in the newspaper. I didn't want to look at the photos, yet I couldn't stop myself from looking at them, reading the obituaries again and again.

News of my daughter's death and my father-in-law's death spread quickly. We received dozens of sympathy cards, endless phone calls, and fragrant bouquets. These gestures were more comforting than I anticipated. Two months passed, and I thought I was doing well until I received a call from my brother.

He lived in Florida. We had been estranged for years—I didn't understand the reasons—so I was surprised to hear from him. We chatted about mundane things for a few minutes, then he announced, "I have tongue cancer, and it has spread to my neck. I wonder if John could get me in to Mayo Clinic in Jacksonville." At the time, John was a physician at Mayo Clinic in Rochester, Minnesota. Of course, my husband agreed to help and made some phone calls. The next day,

John called my brother and told him how to proceed. I knew tongue cancer was difficult to treat but thought my brother would respond to aggressive chemotherapy and survive.

"We'll visit him in a few months," John suggested, "after he is feeling better."

A few months later, my brother called again to say he was almost finished with chemotherapy. He sounded weak to me, maybe even frail, and I began to worry. I worried even more when he declared, "This is the hardest thing I've ever done in my life. I can hardly sit in a chair, let alone walk."

We chatted briefly. When the conversation waned, my brother said, "I love you," and he hung up. A few weeks later, he died of a heart attack. Later, I realized this call had been his final goodbye.

The memorial service for my brother was held in Port Washington, New York. John and I stayed only one night. Our granddaughter was receiving a Girl Scout award the next day, and we promised to be there for the ceremony. The memorial service was painful. Three family members had died within a few months—my daughter, my father-in-law, and my brother—and it was too much to process.

Life was grim. "I don't expect anything to go right anymore," I admitted to John. "All I expect is tragedy."

"Well, I'm afraid this is becoming the norm for us," John admitted. "This is too much tragedy for anyone."

I thought of myself as a strong person, but experiencing multiple losses overwhelmed me. I was stressed, confused, and exhausted.

Grief is personal, and I wondered if I would survive multiple losses. I felt like I'd lost all control over my life. At times, I felt as if I were living someone else's life. Could I be happy again? How would grief change me? What did the future hold? I had many questions, and no answers were in sight.

Well-meaning friends asked me to stop writing and use the time to focus on grief and raise my grandchildren. According to these friends, continuing with my writing career would be difficult and add to my existing stress.

"Don't push yourself so hard," one commented.

Writing wasn't pushing myself. It was my life. If I stopped writing, I would lose myself, and I didn't want that to happen. Therefore, I didn't heed this advice. Instead, I switched from writing about health and wellness to writing about grief healing. Not recovery, because you never recover completely from the death of a loved one.

I searched websites for books that would aid my research. No website had the book I needed: *Multiple Losses for Dummies*. Though I felt dumb, I knew I wasn't dumb. I was devastated by grief. In fact, I could barely function. At the time, I had no inkling there was more grief to come.

In November 2007, eight months after the twins lost their mother in a car accident, their father tragically lost his life in yet another car accident. The circumstances surrounding his death were unbelievable. The town highway department had switched the stop signs at a busy intersection. Cars that previously stopped were now allowed to proceed, and vice versa. This change wasn't widely publicized. A driver had hit my former son-in-law's car broadside and gravely injured him. He died a few hours later.

The *Post Bulletin* newspaper in Rochester, Minnesota, published an article about the intersection, "Death Prompts Intersection Change." The article quoted a town councilman, who said there was "no chance for anybody to be safe" after the stop signs were switched. The death of the twins' father proved his point. I couldn't believe my grandchildren's mother and father had died in the same way, only a few months apart.

Family members were equally stunned. "What is God thinking?" a cousin asked. Friends asked me the same question. Other friends questioned God's plans. One friend went so far as to say God had made a mistake. The twins had lost both parents, and John and I were now in charge of them. At the time, John and I were in our early seventies. Would we have enough energy to parent teenagers again?

The twins moved in with us on the night their father died.

"No offense, but I think living with you will be weird," my granddaughter declared.

Despite the hasty and unusual arrangement, we could still be a family and take care of each other. The twins lived with us for seven years and, as time passed, we became a "grandfamily," a term coined by the American Association of Retired Persons (AARP).

Grief is universal, something people of all races, cultures, and beliefs experience. It reassured me to know I wasn't alone in grief. Writing got me through challenging times, and I learned more about grief than I wanted to know: buying a burial plot, choosing a casket, ordering a headstone, arranging a memorial service, writing an obituary, and suggesting memorials in memory of the deceased.

"Life has made you a grief expert," a colleague remarked.

Though I never dreamed I'd write this book, it's one of the most important books I've ever written because I lived it. *Grief in Your Words* may be an important book for you too.

Whether you're grieving for one loss or several, writing helps, and I hope you tell your grief story. As words accumulate, you may realize you are writing to survive. Writing about grief helps you find your way through it. You don't have to be an author to express your grief with words. Just be yourself. Years from now, your writing will link generations together and be part of your family's history.

Future generations may benefit from your story. Indeed, they may be grateful for it, find strength in it, and draw upon this strength.

You have a story to tell, a unique story that is yours alone. Though grieving people have similar symptoms, nobody's grief is like yours. Your grief is unique. In *Finding Meaning: The*

Sixth Stage of Grief, David Kessler believes that telling our stories helps to heal grief.[1] Writing about grief is a gift to yourself and, in time, may be a gift for others.

As Kessler writes, "In a way, meaning both *begins* and *ends* with the stories we tell."[2]

---

1 David Kessler, *Finding Meaning: The Sixth Stage of Grief* (New York: Scribner, 2019), 45.
2 Kessler, 51.

PART 1

Getting Ready to Write

Writing is medicine.
— **Julia Cameron**

A blank page or document can be scary. Before, you read someone else's words. Now it's up to you to fill the white space, and many questions may come to mind. Should you start with a prompt, a story, or a word? After you've made this decision, you wonder if it's the right one. Just as there is no right or wrong way to grieve, there is no right or wrong way to express feelings with words. You are entitled to your feelings and to express them in your own way.

The Benefits of Writing

One thing is certain: Inside of you, there's a story to be told, and you're the best one to tell it. "I'm not a writer," may be your initial response. That doesn't matter. Sharing grief and getting it out in the open is what matters. The opposite is also true. Holding grief inside—a response grief counselors call "stuffing"—can be harmful to your mind and body.

Stuffing feelings may prolong grief, something you don't want. "If you keep your grief to yourself, you run the unnecessary risk of it becoming distorted," says Bob Deits, author of *Life After Loss*.[3] Grief has already distorted your life, and you don't want to make things worse by hiding your feelings. The words you write help to release feelings and get them out in the open. Seeing words on paper can be a positive, clarifying experience.

Writing has helped to heal grieving people around the world. Though writing can trigger emotions, it gives you a chance to face your feelings, process them, and, if necessary, let them

---

3 Bob Deits, *Life After Loss: A Practical Guide to Renewing Your Life After Experiencing Major Loss* (New York: Hachette Books, 2017), 78.

go. Letting go isn't easy, that's for sure, but it is necessary to move forward with life. As you write, the path to healing becomes clearer—a path that is as unique as your grief.

Surprises happen, and they may make you stray from your healing path. While this is normal, it is worth examination. Writing gives you opportunities to remember happy times with family members and friends—times you hold dear. The more you write, the more helpful writing becomes.

You may write once a week, twice a month—whatever works best for you. Writing has many benefits, and you may as well take advantage of them. Like all who grieve, you're entitled to these benefits. I wrote the following words to summarize the benefits of writing.

When You Write to Heal, You . . .

- Access your conscious and subconscious mind
- Use alone time wisely
- Take a break from life's busyness
- Are being creative
- Try out ideas
- Identify and name feelings
- Weigh pros and cons
- Start to accept reality
- Document family history
- Discover new things about yourself
- Clarify your problems
- Explore possible solutions
- See weaknesses in your support system
- Become aware of the patterns in your life

- Promote mindfulness
- Think about goals and dreams
- Tap religious or spiritual beliefs
- Identify new pathways
- Practice self-care
- Boost your self-worth
- Create a new life

Your mind needs time to process everything that has happened. In a sense, time is on your side.

Joyce Carol Oates and Meghan O'Rourke discuss expressing grief with words. For O'Rourke, writing about grief is an attempt to gain understanding. Oates writes from a different perspective and describes grief writing as an attempt to comprehend it and "keep yourself alive."[4] It sounds like Oates writes to survive grief, and maybe, with lots of self-reflection and grief work, eventually thrive.

Writing can be a transformative experience, a way to document the past, find a path to the future, and become whole again.

---

4 Joyce Carol Oates and Meghan O'Rourke, "Why We Write About Grief," *New York Times*, February 26, 2011, https://www.nytimes.com/2011/02/27/weekinreview/27grief.html.

Choosing the Best Writing Form for You

Write what should not be forgotten.
— **Isabel Allende**

Grief experts, physicians, and counselors often ask clients to write about their grief. This writing takes many forms: diary entries, journal entries, articles, songs, and more. Let's take a closer look at some of these forms.

A diary is a daily record of thoughts and experiences. To keep a diary, you need to be persistent and patient. Day after day, you keep writing.

A journal is a regular, but not daily, record of thoughts and experiences. You write in a journal every few days or every few weeks. This form of writing takes less effort than a diary.

An article is a focused narrative on a topic. Articles include interviews, quotes, reference citations, and opinions. If you're interested in writing articles for free, consider reaching out to Open to Hope, the Compassionate Friends, or the Grief Toolbox. You can find their contact info in the "Support for You" section at the end of this book.

If you're musical, you can write a song. Eric Clapton wrote "Tears In Heaven" in memory of his four-year-old son, Conor, who died after falling from a window. You don't need to be creative in your writing to cope with grief. These are other ways to help your healing.

Gather the financial facts.

These facts may include burial costs, memorial service costs (clergy, musician, food, etc.), as well as the costs of clearing and cleaning your loved one's place, to cite a few. Having the facts will help you make informed financial decisions now and in the future. Instead of making hasty decisions, you did your "homework." Be proud of this accomplishment.

Become a dedicated list maker.

Moorea Seal has written a book about list-writing called *52 Lists for Happiness*. Moorea organizes her lists into categories: Reflect, Acknowledge, Invest, and Transform. These categories are subdivided into smaller prompts. Under the Transform category, for example, the first prompt is "List the things that felt important five or ten years ago but are unimportant now."[5]

Now may be the right time to make two lists: "Things I've Done" and "Things I Hope to Do." Many people call the second list their *bucket list*—stuff they hope to do before they "kick the bucket," as the saying goes. List-writing is a good way to prepare for lengthier writing.

Keep careful, detailed notes.

Notes may be scribbled on an envelope or scrap paper, but they are a form of writing. After my husband died in 2020, I had so many phone calls to make, so I took notes on who I needed to

---

5 Moorea Seal, *52 Lists for Happiness: Weekly Journaling, Inspiration for Positivity, Balance, and Joy* (Seattle: Sasquatch Books, 2016), 14.

call and the points that were discussed. Without these notes, I would have been disorganized, confused, and I may have made poor decisions. A few hasty notes are better than none.

Write down your conversations with others who have experienced grief.

Having conversations like these can help alleviate the feeling of lonliness in your grief, as well as stimulate writing. Did they express their grief in words? What experiences were the hardest for them? Are there similarities between your grief and theirs?

Describe life's simple joys.

Take the time to enjoy the beauty around you. Call "time-out," sit down, and have a cup of coffee or tea. Close your eyes, sit quietly in a chair, let your thoughts wander, and then write about them. Perhaps something happened today that made you happy—receiving a beautiful card, a bouquet of flowers, or phone call from a dear friend. These things are worthy of written documentation.

Writing to cope with grief also doesn't have to be time-consuming. Even small reminders, like sticky notes or one-word emotions written on a calender, can be immensely helpful.

Finding a writing form that works for you involves trial and error. Try one form of writing for a couple of days, another form on another day, and so on. Writing is a good way to release, identify, and cope with feelings. Which writing form suits you best?

Gathering Your Materials

Start writing no matter about what. The water does not flow until the
faucet is turned on.
— Louis L'Amour

Before you start writing, gather the supplies: scratch paper or a notepad, a red pen (or any other color) for corrections, extra ink cartridges and paper for the printer, and some manila folders. The folders aren't necessary, but it's nice to have them on hand to store rough drafts and printouts.

Some people—and Joyce Carol Oates is one of them—prefer to write in longhand. If you prefer longhand, you need a writing instrument that glides easily across the paper. No getting stuck. No spaces or splotches. No stops. This instrument could be your favorite pen, a felt-tip pen, or a soft pencil. However, the words you write are more important than penmanship. The goal is to get your words on paper before you forget them. Storage is important too. When I'm writing an article or book, I keep the pages in a large plastic box with a lid. This protects the pages and keeps them from getting lost. Because I'm a nonfiction author, I file printouts of articles in folders. I also write notes to myself on the articles, such as: "Revise first paragraph on page 27" and "See list of possible words."

After accidentally throwing away several first drafts, I decided to keep them and make notes on them. I may write "SAVE" in big red letters on top of the page. I also keep notes to myself. Important notes and papers are tacked to a bulletin board next to my workstation.

You can also back up your writing on Google Drive. Remember to save your work often. I save my work every half hour, but you may wish to save the document more often. Check to see if books that interest you are available on Kindle, or Audible if you prefer to listen to audiobooks.

Nothing replaces printed words on paper and, because I'm a visual person, I print out rough drafts and finished pages. This gives me an idea of how the words would look in a book, article, or on a web page.

Printed pages also serve as markers of progress. Reading some of my past articles helps me track this progress. I'm reminded of writing techniques that worked well and those that didn't work so well. I come across some of my favorite words that I plan to use again. I think of ways I can improve future writing projects and note them in the page margins.

Other materials you may collect before you start writing are books and articles that give you hope. Over time, I've gathered a small library of grief books, and they take up two shelves of my bookcase. Because I own the books, I write in the margins and tab important pages with sticky notes. I continue to add to my library and learn from other grief authors, including grief books for young children, tweens, and teens.

Having a willingness to write sets the stage for progress and, eventually, healing. Keeping supplies on hand and writing regularly will help you get through this awful and "awe-full" time. Writing your story is a way to honor your loved one and the precious days you shared.

Finding a Place to Write

Writing is a miracle. You can travel to anywhere in the world,
to any time and place—and still be home for dinner.
— Mary Pope Osbourne

Before you start writing, you need two places: a place to think and a place to write. This may sound easy, but finding these places can be difficult.

All writing begins with thinking. Now, take a moment to look around your home and find a comfortable place to think. It could be in the basement, like my early writing days, or in a separate office, at the kitchen table, or even outdoors where you can be close to nature. Your thinking place needs to be a quiet place, away from the hustle and bustle of life.

My thinking place was the couch in the family room, and I sat there every day. The television was on and the sound was off. There were three white birch trees outside the window. Cardinals often landed on the branches and seemed to look at me while I brainstormed. This was the perfect place to prepare for writing.

- I thought about my daughter's short life and everything she accomplished.
- I thought about my daughter's education: an MBA and six engineering certifications.
- I thought about her kindness: homemade apple pies, printing out articles for my research paper and assembling them in a notebook, and making me an embroidered apron.
- I thought about how she slapped her knee when she laughed heartily. Her laughter made me laugh.
- I thought about her dream to be the best composite engineer she could be.
- I thought about the new man who had come into her life after her divorce, a man she loved and planned to marry.
- I thought about her twins—my precious grandchildren—and vowed to love them more each day.

My thinking place was perfect, and I spent many hours there. This thinking place led to dozens of articles and books.

Once you find your thinking place, whether it's a chair or couch, sit there for a while and let your mind wander. Do this for ten to fifteen minutes over the course of several days. Is the chair comfortable and cozy? Does it inspire you to write about some of the thoughts that come to mind? Change your thinking place if you aren't comfortable.

As your mind wanders, you may think of your childhood, your parents, family members, friends, your education, and the role your deceased loved one played in your life. You may worry about the future and if you will survive without your loved one. What awaits you in life?

I thought about the gaping holes that death had cut from the fabric of my life. I thought about happy relationships and sad ones. I thought about anger and regrets. I thought about the power of love. These thoughts were my homework. Then I went downstairs to my office, booted up the computer, and resumed writing.

After you find a place to think, now you must find a place to write. The place where you write can be just as important as the topics you write about.

When I first started writing forty-five years ago, I wrote in a combination guest room and office. For a long time, I wrote on an electric typewriter, but it continually malfunctioned and was often in the repair shop. One day, I was so frustrated, and I told the repairman, "I'd like to throw this off a tall building!"

He looked surprised and promised to fix the typewriter within a week. I thanked him, but deep in my heart, I knew I'd be back again next month with my frustrating, undependable typewriter.

To make matters worse, the typewriter was on a rickety rolling stand next to the utility room, always a noisy place. I would hear the hot water heater turn on, the hum of the furnace in the winter, and the air conditioner in the summer. Something always seemed to be running and humming, and there was no escape. It took years to learn how to ignore these sounds. I would type several paragraphs and be briefly satisfied only to be disturbed by the sounds of machinery.

Today, I can write at any time because I have found my writing place after I invested in a dedicated office. I bought a new computer, ergonomic chair, and printer. Now the only sound I hear is the clicking of computer keys.

If you have a computer workstation, make sure the chair is the right height. You also need adequate lighting. Many experts believe the light source should come from the left, but overhead lighting works just as well. I have overhead lighting (can lights) and an extra lamp for gray days and nighttime work.

Writers, including beginning ones, usually have a beverage nearby: coffee, tea, juice, or water. More times than I want to admit, I've spilled coffee all over my notes. Several of my friends ruined their keyboards by accidentally spilling drinks on them. Put your cup or glass on a level spot, well away from the computer.

In addition to a writing and thinking place, you may need a storage space. Keep your writing in a standing file cabinet, portable file holder, or box with a lid. If you're using a computer, you can store your writings in digital folders.

To write, you need to feel physically and emotionally comfortable; otherwise, your mind will be diverted by the discomfort you feel. Think of your writing place as a special place for healing, solace, and dreams.

The Joy of Journal Writing

Fill your paper with the breathings of your heart.
— **William Wordsworth**

Psychotherapist Kathleen Adams from the Center for Journal Therapy says journal writing is "cheap therapy" and helps you track the ebb and flow of life—patterns you may have missed before. "We live a hundred tiny deaths from hour to hour," Adams notes, and "each death leads to rebirth."[6] With the passage of time, your writing may spark rebirth and faith in the future.

According to Adams, there are different kinds of journals: dialogues, character sketches, lists, meditative writing, topic of the day, describing possessions, changes in your body, list-writing, and more. Whether you write phrases, lists, or paragraphs, Adams asks us to remember something

6 Kathleen Adams, *Journal to the Self: Twenty-Two Paths to Personal Growth* (New York: Grand Central Publishing, 1990), 11.

important: "Your journal will log your joy just as faithfully as your pain, your laughter with as much expression as your tears, your triumphs in as much detail as your tragedies."[7]

Many people have asked if I keep a journal. Answering this question is difficult because my books are my journals, filled with personal stories and ideas. Therefore, my reply is, "Each book I write is like a journal." This reply surprises some people, and often prompts a discussion about keeping a journal and the joy of doing it. And journal writing *can* be a joy.

If you get into the right mindset, you can make journal writing a positive experience, filled with the names of relatives, dear friends, helpful strangers, and the happy experiences you've had in your life. Though you may have weighed the pros and cons of writing, you wonder if you should keep a diary or a journal. Which would suit you best?

Christina Baldwin, author of *One to One: Self-Understanding Through Journal Writing*, defines a "diary" as a formal pattern of daily entries that document activities, experiences, and observations.[8]

Daily is the key word here, and it can be a problem. With one loss, or several, there is little time to write in a diary. You may think about making entries or even plan them in your head, but following through may not happen. There's just not enough time, and daily writing seems like a herculean task. This is where journal writing enters the scene.

When you keep a journal, you write *regular* entries and choose an interval that works for you. Journal writing is more casual than diary writing. Baldwin defines a journal as an "intermittent record of an inner life, written consistently, but not necessarily on a daily basis."[9] Baldwin believes a journal is just the place to tuck away snippets of your life. You discover this by what you write and what you learn.

---

7 Adams, 11.

8 Christina Baldwin, *One to One: Self-Understanding Through Journal Writing* (Maryland: M. Evans & Company, 1991) 6–7.

9 Baldwin, 8.

You rediscover yourself.

Adams describes the journal writing process in her article, "Managing Grief through Journal Writing." Adams thinks most people "will open themselves up and pour themselves out onto the page."[10] Though you may write only a few sentences or paragraphs each time, I hope you'll write your grief story.

Open yourself up, pour yourself out, and discover yourself in words. You may also pour out your feelings in articles, poems, books, and talks.

Perhaps you're intimidated by journal writing. If you don't enjoy journaling, you can always change your mind. But your thoughts are worth putting into words. The following tips worked for me, and I hope they will work for you too. Choose a couple of tips and try them. You're off to a stellar start with your grief work.

Journal Writing Tips

- Sit quietly and focus on your thoughts.
- Be aware of thoughts that fly by like birds.
- Decide on the writing forms you want to try.
- Jot down your thoughts as quickly as you can.
- Decide on tense—present or past.
- Don't worry about handwriting, spelling, or punctuation.
- Write for about fifteen minutes, or more if you're on a roll.
- Document happy memories and experiences.
- Include notes to yourself, such as "Write more about stress next time."
- Be honest with your feelings even if they are scary.
- If you can, name your feelings. It's okay if you can't.

10 Kathleen Adams, "Managing Grief through Journal Writing," Journal Therapy, accessed August 9, 2023, https://journaltherapy.com/wp-content/uploads/2015/04/Article-KA-Managing-Grief-through-Journal-Writing.pdf.

Remember, you're not editing your writing. That comes later—if it comes at all. You may decide that no editing or some editing is necessary. That's fine. Change a few words if you must, but don't overdo it. Stick with original thoughts because they come from your soul. When you reach the end of *Grief in Your Words*, you may continue writing in a notebook or in a Word document.

What you think and what you write are girders for the future. You are getting stronger by the day.

Brainstorming About Writing Ideas

Write hard and clear about what hurts.
— **Ernest Hemingway**

Brainstorming topics to write about involves group or individual thinking. Even if you're in shock, you are capable of brainstorming. Sit in a quiet place, close your eyes, let your mind wander, and note the range of ideas that come to mind, including the unusual ones.

Disregard negative thoughts and focus on the positive ones. Be patient with yourself if your mind starts to wander.

A wandering mind is normal. The moment your mind heard the tragic news, you went into fight-or-flight mode. Your mind started to work differently, and your body worked differently too. You may have started to feel some symptoms of grief: sobbing, tight throat, dry throat (from all the tears you shed), headaches, shortness of breath, nausea, poor appetite, no appetite, fatigue, confusion, acute stress, and more.

Some people develop "grief heart" and have symptoms that mimic a heart attack, including chest pain. Chest pains are serious stuff and warrant a 911 call or a visit to the hospital. Writing about symptoms helps you keep track of them. Just as important, your writing can help health professionals help you. Best of all, writing can help you help yourself.

But you may be so stressed right now that you don't think you can write anything. That's understandable. Still, you may ease into writing by following this three-step approach. The approach is simple and, better yet, it works. These steps have helped me brainstorm about writing.

Step 1: Keep a one-word journal on a calendar page (you can download blank calendar pages online). Each day, write one word that describes your feelings. These words may include *stressed, confused, worried, anxious, okay, determined, busy, blessed,* and *hopeful.* Do this for at least a week, two weeks, or even a month.

Step 2: Once you're used to keeping a one-word journal, take the next step and write a sentence a day about your feelings. The sentence doesn't need to be long. A simple sentence like "I'm feeling better today" is fine. Write the sentences on a small notepad or computer file. Date each entry.

Step 3: Write a short paragraph a day. Choose words that describe your feelings and the challenges you face. After you feel comfortable writing a paragraph, write several paragraphs. Again, your paragraphs don't need to be long. Short paragraphs can be revealing and powerful.

Your writing may describe "why" questions: "Why did this happen to my loved one?" "Why did this happen to me?" "Why didn't I do things differently?" These questions are painful to ask and answer.

Ruthanne Reid shares writing ideas in her article, "Show, Don't Tell: How to Write About the Stages of Grief." She has many ideas: writing about denial, writing about social interactions, writing about forgetting your loved one has died, and writing about your fears. "If you take nothing else from this article, take this: if you continue to create while you are grieving, you will survive it better."[11]

The topic or topics you write about don't really matter, according to Adams. "Just remember to have fun, try new things, and enjoy the journey."[12] Perhaps include some funny stories in your writing if you can. You can write about a family picnic, a trip you took, or the humorous stories your loved one told.

My father-in-law had a repertoire of humorous stories and told them again and again. Dad knew he repeated stories and didn't feel bad about it. "I get more pleasure from retelling stories than the displeasure you get from hearing them," he declared confidently. Only Dad could get away with a line like that.

Write about the help you received from family, extended family, dear friends, church members, or neighbors you barely know. International organizations, such as the Compassionate Friends and Open to Hope, may be a source of help and understanding.

Writing about relationships is one idea. Exploring dreams is another. You don't have to write in complete sentences or sentences that make sense, you just need to write. Lists are okay. Repeating stories is okay. Transferring your thoughts to paper is what's important, or as Adams says, "Just get it down!"[13]

As you go forward on your healing path, your tears will be fewer, you will become more observant, and you will start to feel stronger. These are forward steps in your grief journey, worthy of drawing smiley faces on your calendar. The day will come when you feel strong enough to reach out to others who are bereaved. Your words and kindness may help another bereaved person more than you realize.

---

11 Ruthanne Reid, "Show, Don't Tell: How to Write the Stages of Grief," The Write Practice, accessed August 9, 2023, https://thewritepractice.com/writing-grief.

12 Adams, *Journal to the Self,* 23.

13 Adams, *Journal to the Self,* 126.

Can one person make a difference? The answer is a mighty "yes," and that person could be you.

Years ago, I came across a poem, "Just One." The poem's inspiring message—the power of one—stayed in my mind. When I felt down, I read the poem and it would make me feel better. I associated the word "one" with writing because writing was, and continues to be, a solitary experience. You're only one person, but there is strength inside you, and writing your grief story can help you harness it. This poem may be the boost you need.

JUST ONE

One song can spark a moment,
One flower can wake the dream.
One tree can start a forest,
One bird can herald spring.

One smile begins a friendship,
One handclasp lifts a soul.
One star can guide a ship at sea,
One word can frame the goal.

One vote can change a nation,
One sunbeam lights a room.
One candle wipes all darkness,
One laugh will conquer gloom.

One step must start each journey,
One word must start each prayer.
One hope will raise our spirits,
One touch can show you care.

One voice can speak with wisdom,
One heart can know what's true.
One life can make a difference,
That one life could be you.

— **Maryam Kazmi**

PART 2

Readings to Jump-Start Writing

Just write every day of your life. Read intensely. Then see what happens.
— **Ray Bradbury**

This section contains sixteen short chapters on topics that I found useful when writing about my extensive grief experience. I hope these topics resonate with you as much as they do with me.

At the end of each chapter is a writing prompt. After you've read a chapter, don't feel as if you need to respond to the writing prompt immediately. Think about your response for a few hours, a day, or several days. Then, when you're ready, put your thoughts into writing.

The purpose of a prompt is to spark your thinking about different topics to write about. However, you may come across something in your day-to-day life that serves as a writing prompt of its own, such as a family photo that brings up vivid memories, or a conversation with another person that leads you to new ideas about grief. While these ideas can be surprising, you can file these thoughts in your mind and vow to write about them later.

Coping with Grief: Your Mental Toolkit

Coping with grief—trying to handle what life has thrown at you—is a way to improve your life. While not every coping step is successful, at least you tried, and that's something to cheer about. Successful coping hinges on the age of your loved one, how he or she died, when and where the death occurred. Anniversary reactions—the return of grief and tears on certain days—also influence coping.

My daughter's death in 2007 shocked me to the core. She was too young to die, and I felt that nature had made a mistake. I couldn't focus my thoughts and kept losing things. These grief responses were bad enough, but I also became a klutz. Grief turned me into a bumbling, stumbling person, and I was ashamed and annoyed with myself. Bummer.

Fortunately, I had written about grief before. This helped me see where I was on the healing path. I took steps to cope with grief. One of those steps was to create a mental toolkit. The ideas in this toolkit may help you get to the next minute, the next hour, or the next day.

Cry when it's necessary.

In his book, *The Language of Tears*, Jeffrey A. Kottler says we need to give ourselves permission to cry.[14] Let yourself cry anytime, anywhere, for as long as necessary. Crying releases feelings and, after a bout of tears, you might feel better. But there's more to crying. Tears by themselves are hardly helpful, Kottler explains, "unless you are willing to balance the intensity of emotion with the other side of your brain that asks some challenging questions."[15]

Find comfort in friends.

Every phone call, email, and sympathy card is a candle in the darkness. Friends may stop by and give you hugs. Flowers may be delivered to your door. Now isn't the time to worry about sending thank-you notes and emails. Just let friends comfort you. This will make everyone happy.

Find comfort in daily tasks.

Ordinary tasks—laundry, dishes, grocery shopping, cleaning—can be comforting, as they divert the mind and offer mini breaks from grief. It provides some structure for a life that feels like it's falling apart. But you're not falling apart; you are grieving. Being involved in ordinary tasks, such as folding sheets, can be calming and make you feel you've accomplished something.

Get some help.

Help may come from a certified grief counselor or from books written by grief authors. Grief authors write about helpful things. Authors who write about life in general also write about helpful things by sharing glimpses of their lives. Heather Lende, Alaska's writer laureate, is one

---

14 Jeffrey A. Kottler, *The Language of Tears* (New York: John Wiley & Sons, 1996), 175.
15 Kottler, 177.

of these people. I have three of her books: *If You Lived Here, I'd Know Your Name; Take Good Care of the Garden and the Dogs;* and *Find the Good.* Each book helped me on my grief journey.

See the spirit.

Sometimes people don't know what to say to a grieving person, especially a bereaved parent. For me, the most comforting words were "I'm so sorry." You may have received comments that seemed a bit tactless. Ignore them. Focus on the caring behind these comments and thank people for thinking of you. Their concern can be empowering and give you a burst of energy at a time when you need it.

Say your loved one's name.

After a loved one dies, others may not say your loved one's name because they don't want to make you sad. But the death of a loved one leaves a hole in your life. You need to say your loved one's name to keep their spirit alive. Say your loved one's name often. Every time you say their name, think of it as a hug from them.

What tools from your mental toolkit can you use to cope with the death of your loved one?

Receiving the Gift of Food

Delivering food to a grieving family is an honored custom. Though the custom has existed for years, it could use some updating. During this difficult time, you may have received the gift of food. These are my suggestions for improving food delivery.

Be honest with yourself and others.

If someone tells you they are going to deliver food, tell them what time works best for you. If your freezer is full, share this information too. Certainly, if someone in the family has a food allergy, the delivery person needs to know this. You want the gift of food to be a rewarding experience for everyone involved.

Note serving sizes.

Grieving people can lose their appetites. Ask the person who is gifting the food to divide it into small servings and put them in Ziploc bags or freezer cartons. This makes things easier for you, and for them. Write the date on the food you receive.

Freeze what you can for later.

Relatives and friends may deliver so much food you feel like you're running a grocery store. Ask someone to help you clear out the freezer to make room for new food and freeze it for another day. If you have extra food, donate it to a food bank, relative, or neighbor.

Remember to say thank you.

A thank-you can be a short email, a note, or a phone call. Sometimes it helps to have a long chat with a friend who understands and comforts you. On the other hand, you may choose to keep the call short because you have so many things to do. Begin by saying something like, "I have legal stuff to attend to, but I wanted to give you a quick thank-you call. We enjoyed the food immensely. Thanks for thinking of us."

But the best food you can receive is food for the soul: the words "I'm so sorry." These three little words will be remembered and can brighten a grieving person's day.

After your loved one died, did people deliver food to you? What did they deliver? Did you also receive food for the soul?

_____

_____

_____

_____

Setting Goals After a Loved One Dies

After my daughter died, I knew things would never be the same. Yet I had to live my life. How could I go about it? I wanted to move forward, but I was so overwhelmed by grief that I feared I'd get stuck in the past. To prevent this from happening, I set new goals, an intellectual process that made me think about the future.

Daniel Goleman, author of *Emotional Intelligence,* links goal-setting with hope and cites the work of C. R. Snyder. "Snyder defines [hope] with more specificity as 'believing you have both the will and the way to accomplish your goals, whatever they may be.'" [16]

I moved goal setting toward the top of my list of grief healing steps. Though stress made goal-setting difficult, one goal was clear: The moment my daughter died, I dedicated my life to her children—my grandkids. "There must be other goals," I muttered to myself. "Something to occupy my busy, searching mind."

As I made the bed, washed dishes, and folded laundry, I let my mind wander. This went on

16 Daniel Goleman, *Emotional Intelligence: Why It Can Matter More Than IQ* (New York: Random House, 2012), 87.

for several weeks. Suddenly, the fog lifted from my mind. I saw my goals clearly and thought they were good ones. Instead of expressing goals in the future tense, I expressed them in the present tense:

- "I am a role model for my grandchildren and great-grandchildren."
- "I care for myself so I can care for others."
- "I keep some hobbies so I am still me."
- "I help others now that I'm stronger."

This may be a good time for you to set some goals. Your goals may refer to your physical, emotional, and future life. Avoid setting too many goals at once. You may start out with a long list, identify the most important things on it, and choose to work on one or two of them. Write a list of goals and add the date. Revise the list a few weeks later. When you read your list, understand that you are planning a future.

What are two realistic goals you would like to achieve?
What are some manageable steps you can take to achieve them?

_____

_____

_____

_____

_____

_____

Living a Loved One's Values

After a loved one dies, sometimes it's helpful to identify with their values. Doing this keeps your loved one alive in your mind. To free myself from the cold grip of the past, I counted my blessings and thought about values. I strived to pass the family values of hard work, honesty, education, and giving back, from one generation to the next.

Every day without my daughter was a day of tears. My fifteen-year-old grandkids were so overcome with grief for their mother they were almost paralyzed. Still, we shared stories about her, and the twins enjoyed hearing them. But it was the values she instilled in them that helped most. I gave each twin a list of their mother's values.

Your Mother's Values

Family comes first. Your mother found love and support in her family. She wanted the same for you, which is why we had Pampa (the twins' great-grandfather) over for dinner when you visited, and why your mother took you to see him when he was dying. Your mother wanted you to understand that family members always came first.

Get an education. Read your mother's résumé and you will see that she was always learning. She knew that more knowledge would lead her to better jobs and a better life. Sometimes she quoted something I said to her: "Nobody can take your education away from you."

Work hard and do your best. Your mother worked hard for you. She got up at four in the morning, drove two hours to her job, and then two hours home. She bought the house you lived in so you could attend the high school you wanted to attend.

Be a kind and caring person. Your mother believed in kindness. She was a Girl Scout leader and a church volunteer, and she gave back to the community in other ways. Your mother believed sharing kindness led to receiving kindness.

Share with others. There were times in life when your mother didn't have much, but she always shared what she had: extra children's clothing, food (like Christmas cookies and apple pie), and plants. Sharing made your mother feel good inside.

Be honest and ethical. Your mother supervised two manufacturing production lines. A disgruntled employee said he wasn't going to eliminate a bolt from production. She told him this wasn't safe and that she would shut down the assembly line if he didn't include the bolt. The man changed his mind.

Laugh every day. Thanks to *The Big Book* (Alcoholics Anonymous) and the way she lived, your mother laughed often. Laughter energized her and delighted those around her. Your mother would want you to laugh and enjoy the miracle of life.

No matter your age, you may benefit from keeping your loved one's values. Continuing their values makes you feel closer to your loved one and helps you to see a forward path in life. When you translate values into action, you're really saying, "I will always remember you." Each day is a day of loving remembrance.

What were your loved one's values?
Which of these values would you like to hold on to?

_____

_____

_____

_____

_____

_____

_____

_____

_____

_____

_____

The Miracles of Kindness

The kindness of others contributes to healing. You know others are thinking of you and want to help. I have a caregiving personality (you may have one too), and though I do kind things for others, I wasn't prepared for the kindness I received after my daughter died.

My husband and I received dozens of cards. One handmade card with an original poem on the front was especially beautiful. We were touched by the sender's kindness, caring, and talent.

A friend gave me a copy of *Thirst*, a book of poetry by Mary Oliver. The poem "In the Storm" changed my view of kindness. "Kindness—as now and again some rare person has suggested—is a miracle."[17] I'd always thought kindness was a value learned in childhood. This poem helped me see kindness as a miracle of life.

Flowers were another kindness and came in many forms—a single yellow rose in a bud vase, an elegant white arrangement, and multicolored bouquets. Two deliveries stood out

---

17 Mary Oliver, *Thirst* (Boston: Beacon Press, 2006), 62.

from the others. One was a basket of tiny blue blossoms from an organization I belonged to, and another was a terrarium from a neighbor. What thoughtful gifts.

Phone calls were kindness. I received calls from friends in Canada, England, and across the country. Some callers were shocked by our family tragedy and cried as they spoke to me. Their empathy was heartfelt. Judy Tatelbaum writes about receiving help from family members and friends in her book *The Courage to Grieve*. "The supportive encouragement to go on with life can be an essential element in recovery from grief."[18]

One act of kindness—a small miracle—can keep you walking toward tomorrow.

What acts of kindness have you received from others?
Which one touched you the most deeply?

_____

_____

_____

_____

_____

_____

_____

_____

---

18 Judy Tatelbaum, *The Courage to Grieve: The Classic Guide to Creative Living, Recovery, and Growth Through Grief* (New York: HarperCollins, 2009), 43.

Time is Different When You're Grieving

When you're grieving, you're acutely aware time is ticking away, whether it's on an antique, wind-up, or digital clock. The passage of time is relentless, but it feels different when you're grieving. Some days, you may feel you don't have enough time. Other days, time may feel like it's moving backward. Time hasn't changed, but your perception of time has.

I hadn't thought about time until a well-meaning friend said, "Last year was hard for you." She was referring to my daughter's death three months before. I didn't understand how we could have such different, indeed drastic, perceptions of time. My friend seemed to be racing toward the future, whereas I seemed to be stuck in the past. We lived in different time zones.

My daughter was born on the twenty-third day of the month and died on the twenty-third day of the month. I winced every time I saw "23" on the calendar. The memories of my daughter as a baby, toddler, elementary student, high school student, and college student were as clear as if it were yesterday.

Time can seem irregular when you remember the past and worry about the future—things that can keep you awake in the middle of the night. These thoughts may make you anxious. One way to counter anxiety is to think about the special times in your life—birthdays, holidays, family picnics, getting a dog—and find comfort in them. Memories can't bring your loved one back, but they can strengthen you for the future.

Your loved would want you to enjoy the rest of your life. Activate the power within you to create new, vital, happy memories for yourself. Start now.

Does time seem slower or faster right now? What memories about your loved one do you spend the most time thinking about? What worries you about the future?

_____

_____

_____

_____

_____

_____

_____

_____

_____

_____

The Benefits of Exercise

Exercise offers both physical and psychological benefits. Even short exercise spurts—ten or fifteen minutes—can improve your mood. If you make it a goal to exercise even that much, you're heading in the right direction. In the book *How to Go On Living When Someone You Love Dies*, Therese A. Rando says exercise helps reduce the aggressive feelings associated with grief.[19]

Even if you don't have any aggressive feelings, it's wise to stay active. When I have a problem, I go for a short walk or ride a mile on an exercise bike. Afterward, the solution of the problem usually comes to mind. I feel better physically and emotionally, and I'm ready to take some proactive steps or tackle a new problem.

Successive deaths in the family brought my healthy habits to a halt. After being an active walker for years, I dropped my walking program. During the early stages of grief, I reverted to the old habit of comfort food. Grief had turned me into a blob, and something had to be done about it.

19 Therese A. Rando, *How to Go On Living When Someone You Love Dies* (New York: Random House, 1991), 56.

One morning I got up, clipped my pedometer to my waist, and went for a walk. But instead of easing back into my walking program, I walked 9,552 steps and my legs ached the next day. I'd even forgotten to do my stretching exercises beforehand. Don't make the same mistake I did.

Is physical activity part of your day? Walking is cheap exercise and, most importantly, beneficial for your heart. Buy a pedometer and make walking a daily activity. Walk outside when the weather is nice or in a mall when the weather is nasty. Think about your deceased loved one as you walk and picture happy memories in your mind.

Treasure these memories and walk your way to a new life.

What exercise options are you willing to try? What equipment do you need? Remember: vacuuming, gardening, and casual sports like kickball all count as exercise.

Having a Relationship with the Deceased

Grief experts say you need to create a new relationship with a deceased loved one. How can you do this if your loved one is gone? While this question is a conundrum, it can be solved. According to Therese A. Rando, PhD, developing a new relationship with your loved one helps to keep them "alive."[20]

While I understood Rando's point, the word "relationship" confused me, so I looked it up in the dictionary. *Relationship* is defined as being related, a state of affairs between those having relations or dealings, and a romantic or passionate attachment.[21] I'd always thought of a relationship as live interaction, and that wasn't possible anymore. This thought really bothered me.

I expected to see my loved one and for them to see me.

I expected to talk with my loved one and for them to reply.

I expected to see different emotions on their faces.

20 Rando, *How to Go On Living*, 234–237

21 Merriam-Webster, s.v. "relationship (n.)," https://www.merriam-webster.com/dictionary/relationship.

I expected to laugh with my loved one.

I expected to share plans with my loved one and for them to add ideas.

I expected to spend special days with my loved one.

These were unrealistic expectations. "To have a relationship with the deceased, you must have a clear image of him [or her]."[22] Rando says the image has to be realistic and include the flaws that all people have. This was where I ran into trouble. My daughter's childhood was difficult, my father-in-law had memory disease, and my brother and I were estranged. What could I do?

I read the relationship sections of Rando's book again, and two points stood out from the others. The first point is that your loved one is dead and you are alive. The second point is that we, as bereaved people, need to decide which parts of our old lives with our loved ones should be retained. In other words, we find ways to keep loved ones alive in our minds. Rando offers suggestions for doing this, including displaying mementos, eating your loved one's favorite dessert, telling their jokes, quoting your loved one, living their values, and keeping some of the rituals you shared.

These are just a few ways you can keep your loved one alive. Doing this is a healthy, respectful thing to do. "Since [your loved one] was a special part of you and vice versa, you actually are a part of [them] that continues to exist in the world despite [their] death."[23] I've thought about this statement many times since my husband John died in 2020. I truly understand, on a gut level, that John is part of me, and this is empowering. Sometimes I ask myself, "How would John answer this question?"

Knowing that John is a part of me makes me feel stronger. Though he isn't present physically, I still feel like John "has my back," as the saying goes. Of course, there have been times when I had to give myself pep talks, and I was okay with that. In my mind, taking the time for a pep talk was similar to warming up the car engine in wintertime. When I was warmed up, I was ready to

22 Rando, 234.

23 Rando, *How to Go On Living*, 237.

head out and meet the world. After John died, I felt stronger with each passing year. I also felt happier. Happiness was within my reach, and I grabbed it.

It also helped me to hear Tatelbaum's words: "We are recovering when we can look at life ahead as worth living."[24] With full recovery, Tatelbaum says, "We will look back and know that we have fully grieved and survived life's darkest hours."[25] You may feel enveloped by darkness, but I can assure you that there is light ahead.

Developing a different relationship with your deceased loved one is a sign of healing. Though this takes time and effort, you can do it. As life goes on, keep your loved one close to your heart.

How can you develop a new relationship with your loved one?
What values, routines, or quotes would you keep?

---

24 Tatelbaum, *Courage to Grieve*, 94–95.
25 Tatelbaum, *Courage to Grieve*, 94–95.

Honor a Loved One with Their Favorite Dinner

Food brings people together. A food event can be a summer picnic, campout grub, or a fancy dinner. Nothing brought my father-in-law more pleasure than having dinner with his family. He was even happier when we had one of his favorite dinners: grilled steak, French dip sandwiches, Swedish meatballs, and liver and onions (not my favorite).

After he passed away, our family decided to have a memorial dinner with some of Dad's favorite foods: Kentucky Fried Chicken, mashed potatoes and gravy, coleslaw, smoked oysters on crackers, cheese, fresh fruit (for a few vitamins), chocolate-marshmallow cookies, and ice cream. Though this wasn't the healthiest meal, it was pure Dad, especially the gooey cookies.

As family members arrived, they were greeted by a large photo of Dad. I'd typed a list of his favorite sayings that revealed his personality, ethics, and humor. Each guest received a copy of this list:

"After age forty, you should back up your car as little as possible."

"Take credit for what you do."

"This is going to be the best trip ever!"

"Money spent on education is never wasted."

"I don't want to be *neat-enized*." (His word for tidying his apartment.)

The dinner ended with a slideshow of photos of him throughout his life, which sparked tears and laughter.

Consider planning a favorite foods dinner in honor of your loved one. Fix their favorite foods, invite family members to contribute, and add some fun and special meaning. Then sit around the table and tell stories about the person you knew and loved so much. That's what my family did and members enjoyed sharing their memories of Dad. Some stories were funny and others made us cry.

Make a list of your loved one's favorite foods. When did you enjoy these foods together? Describe an event, the setting, the people, and the food.

_____

_____

_____

_____

_____

_____

Got Grief Brain?

Throughout the grieving process, you may experience forgetfulness, confusion, and stress. This is called "grief brain." It is also known as "widow's brain" and "grief fog." Despite the progress I'd made in the recovery process, I was often forgetful. In fact, I was so forgetful that I had to make a list of grief-related phone calls (US Air Force, the church secretary, our lawyer, credit card companies, etc.). This list helped me keep track of what was discussed during these calls.

The calls involved giving and receiving information. You may have discovered that it is painful to make these phone calls. Grief brain can impede logic, decision-making, memory function, and word retrieval. For me, word retrieval was the worst. I knew the word I wanted to say had four letters, but I couldn't think of the word. Whether it was verbal or written, grief brain made communication difficult for me.

I was dealing with communication problems, information problems, and life problems at the same time. Perhaps you are dealing with these things as well. How should we proceed? What should we do if we have grief brain? What shouldn't we do? Psychologist J. William Worden's suggestions may be helpful. Worden says bereaved people dealing with grief brain have four main tasks:

1. Accept the reality of the loss.
2. Process the pain of grief.
3. Adjust to a world without your loved one.
4. Find an enduring connection with that person.[26]

While you know your loved one has died, accepting this emotionally may take some time. Since your grief is unique, you will process it in your own way. Adjusting to a world without your loved one involves finding a new identity and perhaps a new mission in life. Finding a lasting connection with your loved one can be a huge challenge.

That's a tall order for anyone. But there's more work for you to do as you confront the following challenges. You may choose to write about each challenge as you tackle it.

Needing to Let Go

Knowing this and doing it are two different things. Grieving people let go of companionship, conversation, eating together, shared humor, and emotional support. The lack of these things is difficult to accept when you're coping with grief brain. You have good days, bad days, and days where you don't know how you feel.

Constantly Playing Catch-Up

Just when you think you're caught up with your to-do list, you realize you're behind. Rando says that grief makes us less effective and productive, which is natural. "For a while it will be

---

26 "Worden's Four Tasks of Mourning," Our House Grief Support Center, accessed June 11, 2023, https://www. ourhouse-grief.org/grief-pages/grieving-adults/four-tasks-of-mourning/.

impossible for you to function at exactly the same level after major loss as before," explains Rando. "You are just too overwhelmed with psychological, social, and physical responses to that loss."[27]

These words described me and may describe you. Thankfully, Rando offers some practical advice: Don't make major decisions too soon, get some support, think through decisions, and get feedback from those you trust.[28]

When have you experienced "grief brain"? How are you coping with it?

_____

_____

_____

_____

_____

_____

_____

_____

_____

_____

---

27 Rando, _How to Go On Living_, 39.
28 Rando, 39.

When Does the Crying Stop?

It's normal to cry after a loved one dies. Throughout my own grieving process, I couldn't stop crying even when I tried. According to grief expert Jeffrey A. Kottler, we need to give ourselves permission to cry.[29] Let yourself cry anytime, anywhere, for as long as necessary. Crying releases feelings and, after a bout of tears, you might feel better. But there's more to crying. Tears by themselves are hardly helpful, Kottler explains, "unless you are willing to balance the intensity of emotion with the other side of your brain that asks some challenging questions."[30]

Those who are grieving cry at different times and for a myriad of reasons. I cried for months after my daughter died. Once I started crying, I was well into it, and it took hours for my tears to subside. I asked the same question many grievers have: When does the crying stop?

The answer to this question happens with the passage of time. While you may be sick and tired of crying, keep in mind that tears are a reality check. Be patient with yourself, as crying

---

29 Kottler, *Language of Tears*, 175.
30 Kottler, 177.

gradually stops. Your tears will dwindle as you begin to accept death. How will you know this has happened? According to Rando, many factors help crying to cease, and they include:

- A decline in your grief symptoms.
- The ability to talk about your loved one without crying.
- The knowledge that you lead the pain. It doesn't lead you.
- The return of self-esteem.
- No longer avoiding painful thoughts.
- Feeling a kinship to others who are bereaved.
- Looking forward to the future and planning it.
- Finding new meaning in life.[31]

Finally, consider the words of former Israeli Prime Minister Golda Meir, who once said, "Those who do not know how to weep with their whole heart don't know to laugh either." I wept with my whole heart and felt better afterward. Weep with your whole heart and it will heal.

Think about your bouts of crying. Are they frequent or have they slowed down? How does crying help you?

_____

_____

_____

_____

_____

31 Rando, *How to Go On Living*, 284–285.

Coping with Anniversary Reactions

As the anniversary of your loved one's death approaches, you may experience an "anniversary reaction." According to the Mayo Clinic, an anniversary reaction is a return of strong feelings on the anniversary of your loved one's death, or on special days that remind you of them.[32]

Every year, I worried about the anniversary reactions that lay ahead of me. Thanksgiving, Christmas, and birthdays sparked painful memories, and they were discouraging. The grief can often feel as strong as it did the moment you received the news that your loved one has died. The return of these feelings is not necessarily a setback in the grieving process.[33]

However, the anniversary of a loved one's death can provide many opportunities for emotional healing. It is especially helpful when you know what to expect from an anniversary reaction. What might you expect?

Many people have bad dreams, and you may be one of them. Because life has changed so

32 Dana Sparks, "Grief: Coping with Reminders After a Loss," Mayo Clinic News Network, December 29, 2020, https://newsnetwork.mayoclinic.org/discussion/grief-coping-with-reminders-after-a-loss.
33 Sparks, "Coping with Reminders."

drastically, you may feel anxious. Unhappy memories may return and, as hard as you try, you can't seem to erase them from your mind. You may feel angry about your loved one dying as well.

Some people try to avoid anniversary reactions and treat the day as ordinary. "Even for these people, it can be helpful to learn about common reactions that they or their loved ones may encounter so they are not surprised if the reactions occur."[34]

Rando says anniversary reactions are normal and there is no right or wrong way to handle them.[35] This inspired me to come up with an anniversary reaction plan. This is what my plan looked like and it may help you.

- Confront feelings head-on.
- Ask for help.
- Accept help.
- Focus on the positives in my life.
- Plan an activity for the day.

Having a plan eased my anxiety. As painful as anniversary reactions can be, remember they happen because you loved someone—and that's one of life's greatest miracles. This can be empowering. You were loved, and you are still loved. Let love guide you as you create your future.

What anniversary reactions have you experienced?
How did you respond? What is your anniversary reaction plan?

_____

_____

34 "Anniversary Reactions to a Traumatic Event: The Recovery Continues," MentalHelp.net,. accessed May 25, 2023, https://www.mentalhelp.net/ptsd/anniversary-reactions-to-a-traumatic-event.
35 Rando, *How to Go On Living*, 78.

Answering the Question "How are You?"

In the early stage of grief, answering the question "How are you?" can almost feel impossible. Raw, searing, and intensely painful feelings may surface without warning. Grief is constantly playing hide-and-seek. You never know when grief will appear and take you by surprise.

Answering the question "How are you?" may make you sad, and you may be tired of it. Though this is a common question, the timing is usually wrong, and it's asked too soon. Judith R. Bernstein discusses timing in *When the Bough Breaks*. "Just as you can't teach a child to walk before his muscles are ready," she writes, "you can't force the mending to proceed before the mourner is ready."[36] Many people, as much as they care and want to help, don't realize they are asking this question too soon.

When people ask how you are, it's wise to have a prepared answer. These short answers worked for me, and I think they will work for you.

---

36 Judith R. Bernstein, *When the Bough Breaks: Forever After the Death of a Son or Daughter* (Kansas City: Andrews McMeel Publishing, 1998), 21.

"Fine."

This is the easy answer. Americans must say this millions of times a day because it's expected. Of course, you're not fine, but this answer may be helpful. Saying "fine" also allows you to cut the conversation short and be on your way.

"I'm okay."

This answer fits all situations. When you say "okay," people may look relieved. Besides, this answer implies you're holding your own, and maybe you are. Holding your own makes you feel better and each day you feel more "okay."

"Getting along."

This answer is suitable in the middle stage of grief. The word "along" implies progress and shows you're moving forward with life. That's a good thing for you and the person you're talking to and they may look relieved. If you're getting along, they can move along.

"I'm coping."

This is an honest answer, an admission that you need to cope with grief. Because this reply can lead to a serious conversation, it's best to only use it with relatives and close friends. The people who know you well may provide valuable feedback. You may get involved in a conversation about the coping steps that worked best for you and them.

"I'm good."

Use this reply when you're out of the grief woods. You may be good and moving forward on your healing path. When you gaze in a mirror, you may see a person who looks better and feels better. You can, in all honesty, say you're feeling good.

Having answers to "How are you?" is a proactive step. If a conversation gets too painful or lasts too long, you can always claim you're late for an appointment. And you are—an appointment with life.

How do you currently answer the question: "How are you?"
How do others respond? What are other answers you can consider giving?

_____

_____

_____

_____

_____

_____

_____

_____

_____

_____

Creating a Memory Cookbook

After a loved one dies, some people make quilts from their loved one's clothes. Others compile memory books. I did something different for my family and made a memory cookbook. My sister-in-law and I looked through the recipe boxes that belonged to my mother-in-law, whom we called "Nana." We found handwritten recipes, newspaper and magazine clippings, and many duplicates.

The recipes brought back memories of family picnics, holiday dinners, and snacks Nana had prepared for her three growing boys. I typed the recipes, slipped them into plastic sleeves to protect them, put them in a three-ring binder, and titled it: *Favorite Recipes from Nana's Recipe Boxes.* I added a photo of Nana to the cover. There were twenty-five recipes in total. I also wrote a short introduction, which included a story that is still fresh in my mind.

Nana always served Sunday dinner at 1:00 p.m. One day, she announced supper would be cake and ice cream. I laughed because I thought Nana was kidding. But Nana, the only person I've ever known who ate cold butter rolled in sugar, had a sweet tooth. Supper was just as advertised. We had huge bowls of French vanilla ice cream and hefty slices of yellow cake with penuche frosting.

Because the cookbook was a glimpse of family history, I typed the recipes as Nana had written them, including "refrig" for *refrigerator* and references to family members and friends. I made copies of the cookbook, tucked rubber spatulas inside, wrapped them, tied measuring spoons to the top, and gave them to family members on Christmas morning. A few fancy gifts were exchanged, but my homemade cookbooks were the hit of the day. Family members told stories about Nana as they paged through the cookbook.

If you're looking for a meaningful way to remember a loved one, consider making a memory cookbook. My favorite recipe is Nana's fudge. In honor of her memory, I would like to share the recipe with you, just as she wrote it.

Nana's Fudge, 1920

2 cups sugar

1 Tbsp butter

2 squares unsweetened chocolate

¾ cup milk

1 tsp vanilla extract

½ tsp salt

½ cup nuts

Mix INGREDIENTS 1, 2, 3 . . . in a pan on medium-high heat. When it boils up once, lower the heat to a slow boil. After 5 minutes, begin testing for the soft-ball stage (½ tsp fudge in a saucer of ice water). When you can pick up a soft ball in three fingers, it's ready. Cook it one minute more. Remove from stove and cool completely before stirring. Add vanilla, salt, and nuts, and beat until it looks [like] glass and begins to set. Pour into a square cake pan. Cut when hard. (If it gets too hard, add a few drops of cream at the end of the beating.) Cut, enjoy. Be a good scout and clean up the kitchen afterward.

What recipes would be in your loved one's memory cookbook?
What would the categories include?

Giving Yourself Permission to Laugh

For those who are grieving, laughter seems as distant as a foreign land. Even if you have a reputation as a funny person, you may doubt you'll ever laugh again. When this happens, it's time to give yourself permission to laugh. You were worthy of laughter before and will be worthy of it again. I guarantee it.

My friends thought I was funny and encouraged my comments. One friend said I could be a stand-up comedian, a role I never considered. After my husband died, I didn't feel like laughing. This was a painful realization because my husband and I used to laugh every day. Our shared laughter was part of loving each other. But death had changed things, and life wasn't funny anymore. I thought bursting into laughter would be disrespectful to John, yet I missed laughter and the feeling it gave me.

My view of laughter changed after I read an article called "Stress Relief from Laughter? It's

No Joke." Laughter has short-term benefits: increasing oxygen intake; stimulating the heart, lungs, and muscles; and increasing endorphins, the feel-good chemicals in the brain.[37]

There are even more benefits to laughter. It can ease pain, increase personal satisfaction, and improve one's mood. Laughter is the best medicine. So, I gave myself permission to laugh. This permission included several steps:

First, I said the funny things that came into my mind aloud. Frankly, I was nervous about doing this, but I did it anyway. People laughed at my quips and I laughed with them. Laughing made me feel better. Sometimes the effects of a good laugh lasted for hours.

Second, I remembered funny experiences John and I had shared. Once, when we were in our forties, we were visiting his parents in St. Paul, and we started sharing stories. The stories made us laugh. The more we laughed, the louder we became, and we wondered if we were keeping his parents awake. The next morning, I apologized to my mother-in-law for our loud laughter.

"You didn't bother me at all," she said. "Hearing your laughter was wonderful and made me smile."

Third, since laughter released tension, I read funny books and watched television sitcoms, which helped me cope with the stress of grief. Reruns of the *Carol Burnett Show* made me laugh as much as when I first saw them. I thought of the shows when I wasn't watching television and smiled.

Grief is no laughing matter, yet you can still give yourself permission to laugh. Your loved one would want you to laugh freely. Every time you laugh, dedicate your laughter to them. Remember your loved one with a smile. If possible, find a photo of you and your loved one smiling together. Hang the photo where you will see it often.

---

37 "Stress Relief from Laughter? It's No Joke," Mayo Clinic, July 29, 2021, https://www.mayoclinic.org/healthy-lifestyle/stress-management/in-depth/stress-relief/art-20044456.

When was a time you laughed with your loved one?
What made you laugh? Think about all the other laughs you've shared with them.

Be Grateful for Writing

You don't need to be a novelist, biographer, nonfiction author, or poet to benefit from writing. The benefits begin when you pick up a pencil or pen, and they continue to accrue as you write. In a few weeks or months from now, these benefits will become clear, and you will be grateful. That happened to me.

Days after my daughter and father-in-law died, I wrote articles about grief healing for a website. Writing the articles made me feel better, and I wondered why. What was it about writing that changed my thinking? How did writing help me? How can it help you?

Writing makes you focus.

When you're writing, you focus on a topic, string letters together to make words, and use the words to describe something. You can write about how busy you are, or how to fill your day with activities that bring you joy. Maybe you just want to sit on a park bench for an hour and watch people go by. There's one caution, however. Becoming too busy can lead to the avoidance of grief, which can be harmful to you emotionally and physically. The only way to survive grief is go through it. Writing can help you discover a balanced approach between staying busy and being restful.

Writing changes your thinking.

As you remember your life with your loved one, think of the happy times you shared: going to the beach, enjoying a movie, planning a birthday party, buying holiday gifts, and more. If you work at it, you will be able to counter sad thoughts with happy ones, and this can make you stronger. Try to fill your mind with happy memories. Look at photos of happy times if you have them.

Writing keeps your skills sharp.

In some ways, writing is like speaking a different language. You use punctuation, spelling, grammar, and learn new words. When you've finished writing, your language skills are evident on the page. You may be surprised at what you've written. Though you may not be a published author, you are a writer and can be proud of your efforts. The words you've chosen tell a story and express feelings, two things that help with grief healing.

Writing fosters creativity.

Being creative is satisfying. You may be a knitter, singer, or piano player. Writing is also a creative activity, one that involves choosing words from memory, learning new words, stringing words into sentences, checking the logic, flow, and sequence of ideas. Creativity can be an expression of grief or a break from it. For example, I can get so involved in writing that I forget the time and temporarily forget my problems.

Writing keeps you moving forward.

Keep writing to learn more about yourself. Review the things you knew and things you didn't know, such as caregiving skills and organizational skills. Several months from now, read what you first wrote about. Consider how far you're come since then. Like all who grieve, you are a work in progress. Seeing words on paper are proof of that progress. Whether you use a pencil, pen, or computer, be grateful for writing and the ability to express yourself.

What aspects of writing are you grateful for?
How has writing helped you on your grief journey?

_____

_____

_____

_____

_____

_____

_____

_____

_____

PART 3

Finishing the Job

The title of this section doesn't mean you're finished with writing forever. Rather, it means you're stopping for a while to look back at what you've written. Seeing where you've come from helps you understand where you're going. To do this, you need to review your writing. You've changed so much on your grief journey that you may not recognize the person described in your early writings.

Maybe you didn't even write in complete sentences, and just managed to get the gist of your thoughts on paper. That's okay. Pay attention to descriptions of the stages of grief, any themes or patterns that emerge, signs of progress, and glimpses of the future. You are growing as a person and as a writer. Reviewing now can make future writing easier.

Reviewing Your Words

I write because I don't know what I think until I read what I say.
— Flannery O'Connor

Put your writing away for a few weeks. Stash the pages in a drawer or a box with a lid. If you're using a computer, set it aside in a digital folder. Don't think about your writing for a while. Give your mind time to process what you've written. After the break, it's time to review your writing. What do you see? You may have described the stages of grief. You may have written about an experience time and time again. You may have explored relationships—the good, not so good, and the shaky. You may have admitted your fears. You may have outlined your dreams.

When you review your writing, don't worry about typos or grammatical errors. Instead, try to answer the following questions. If you can't answer all of them, that's okay.

- Did I ask for help?
- Did family members and friends help me?

- Do I see problems I didn't see before?
- Can I identify possible solutions to these problems?
- What action steps did I take?
- What action steps can I still take?
- Will these actions make a difference?
- Have I thought about my future?
- How would I rate my mental health?
- Is laughter part of life again?
- Does my life have the same purpose or a new one?
- What does writing reveal about my thinking?

Some answers to these questions may surprise you. Time can change perception markedly. Things that worried you before may now seem less important. For this reason alone, writing about grief is worth the effort. Think of the challenges you've written about, such as planning a memorial service. When you feel stronger, you may share your writing with others. After you have finished a section or filled a notebook, you may start a new writing project.

You've responded to the writing prompts in "Readings to Jump-Start Writing" the best you can. Now you may want to write about other topics, and that's your right as a writer. There are extra pages at the end of this book for you to continue expressing yourself.

Writing about your loved one doesn't eliminate grief, but it does make the process easier to understand. Sharing feelings can also ease the stress that comes with grief. The loss of a loved one will always be with you. Though you may never fully recover from the loss, you can reconcile it, walk forward on your healing path, and honor your loved one in many ways. Grief is hard work, and you're doing that work.

Writing and Personal Growth

Don't go through life, grow through life.
— **Eric Butterworth**

Seeing words on paper can lead to personal growth. The words you choose may help you differentiate from your heart (emotions) and head (rational mind). Writing can increase your "emotional intelligence," a term that Daniel Goleman talks about in his book on grief. "These two minds, the emotional and the rational, operate in tight harmony for the most part, intertwining their very different ways of knowing how to guide us through the world."[38]

As words accumulate, you may begin to see evidence of your emotional mind, rational mind, and personal growth. Of the three, personal growth may be the most important. The awareness of personal growth is like fog lifting on a damp, gray morning. At first you only see fuzzy shapes through the haze. As the fog dissipates, you start to see outlines and details. Finally, you see clear images—your growth and change. What kinds of changes might you expect?

---

38 Goleman, *Emotional Intelligence*, 9.

You learn to categorize your thoughts.

A mental exercise may help you sort things out. Group your thoughts into three categories: *unimportant, rather important,* and *very important.* Discard the unimportant stuff, put aside the rather important stuff, and focus on the important issues. Put these thoughts in writing if you think that will be helpful.

You develop the ability to assess emotions.

In her article, "10 Steps to Heal Your Grief," Roe Ziccarello describes the anger she felt after the death of her son. She kept a grief journal and wrote through her shock, depression, and emotional numbness. Later, when she read her journal, Ziccarello says her anger, blame, and pain almost jumped off the page and grabbed her by the throat, but she was able to harness her pain. She writes: "Chronicling the journey has allowed me to assess my own grief work."[39]

You become more sensitive.

Even if you were sensitive before, grief makes you a more sensitive person. Later, when you feel stronger, you think about helping others and act on this thought. "The best way to cope with sorrow is to console another."[40] Give the gift of listening to a grieving friend, volunteer in memory of your loved one, donate to a medical organization—anything that makes you feel better.

You plan for emotional tune-ups.

As you walk your healing path, you realize you need to think about your feelings, name them, and determine what to do with them. I call this an "emotional tune-up." To arrange one, sit in

---

39 Roe Ziccarello, "10 Steps to Heal Your Grief," Trans4mind, accessed April 27, 2023, https://trans4mind.com/counterpoint/index-emotional-intelligence/ziccarello.html, 8-B.

40 Vamik D. Volkan and Elizabeth Zintl, *Life After Loss: The Lessons of Grief* (New York: Taylor & Francis, 2018), 25.

a comfortable chair. Eliminate background noise if you can. Let your thoughts wander for at least a half hour. Then name your feelings and listen to your soul.

You know your time is limited.

Knowing that your time is limited makes life more meaningful. Rabbi Harold S. Kushner writes about this in his book *When Bad Things Happen to Good People*. "It matters that we choose to read a book or visit a sick friend instead of going to the movies, precisely because we don't have time to do everything."[41] Kushner also says the God he believes in "gives us the strength to cope with the problem."[42] That problem includes grief. Kushner's viewpoint has comforted me many times and prompted me to help others.

You turn to religious or spiritual beliefs.

Faith can help you heal from tragedy, according to Dr. Robert L. Veninga, author of *A Gift of Hope*. When tragedy strikes, we want to run away, Veninga explains. Since there is no place to run, we turn to faith. "Faith has a powerful effect in helping people recover a sense of balance, tranquility and hope."[43] You may write about your faith, spirituality, and mindfulness.

Writing from the heart takes courage. The more you write, the more you build up your courage. And as your courage builds up, the more beautiful life becomes. You are alive. You are a source of family history and role model for family members. Today is your day, a day to write your story.

---

41 Harold S. Kushner, *When Bad Things Happen to Good People* (New York: Knopf Doubleday Publishing, 2004), 87.
42 Kushner, 140–141.
43 Robert L. Veninga, *A Gift of Hope: How We Survive Our Tragedies* (New York: Random House, 1996), 210.

Self-Care Steps

Breathe. Let go. And remind yourself that this very moment is
the only one you know you have for sure.
— Oprah Winfrey

Grief steals your sense of control. Regaining control is a slow, painful process. You grieve for your loss or losses, come to terms with the past, grapple with the present, worry about the future, keep up with daily chores, take care of others, and, if you have time, take care of yourself. Whew!

How can you do these things? You can take the self-care steps detailed in this chapter. These steps are listed in categories: physical, emotional, social, family, and recreational. Self-care steps are necessary for you to heal.

As Judith Viorst explains in *Necessary Losses*, "It becomes increasingly clear that the person in charge of us is . . . us, and we may resent the responsibility."[44] Rather than wasting time on resentment, it's wiser to practice self-care. Not practicing self-care makes grief worse and prolongs it, two things you don't need. Please remember, and believe with all your heart, that you are worthy of self-care.

Each step brings you closer to happiness. Reading this book is a self-care step. Growing older made me realize that happiness isn't something we chase or find; it's something we create. You have the power to choose happiness. When you make this decision, everything in life shifts. Everything looks different because reality is different.

You do things you never thought you would do.

You say things you never thought you would say.

You dream things you never thought you would dream.

Step by step, you walk forward on your healing path. According to Heather Stang, author of "9 Self-Care Tips for Grief," taking one or two self-care steps can help you. Stang's advice is to start with a few "doable" steps. Then try another step in a few days, then another, and another. "Treat yourself as you would treat a beloved friend."[45]

Write about the self-care steps you've taken or hope to take some day. Like baby steps, your first steps may be wobbly and unsure. Will you stumble and fall? Will you hurt yourself? Where are you headed? Don't worry. Self-care steps are seeds of hope. As you nurture them, the seeds burst open and grow toward the light of healing. Writing about the self-care steps you take—and grief writing in general—can lead to renewal and the life you deserve.

---

44 Judith Viorst, *Necessary Losses: The Loves, Illusions, Dependencies, and Impossible Expectations that All of Us Have to Give Up in Order to Grow* (New York: Simon & Schuster, 2010), 142.

45 Heather Stang, "9 Self-Care Tips for Grief: Reduce Your Suffering in Mind, Body & Spirit," Mindfulness and Grief, September 13, 2021, https://mindfulnessandgrief.com/9-self-care-tips-for-grief.

The Steps

Physical

- Listen to your body. If you have new or odd symptoms, seek help from a health care professional.
- Consult with a primary care physician when necessary.
- Take a twenty-minute walk each day. You'll feel better for it.
- Watch for symptoms of grief brain and note them on the calendar.

Emotional

- Cry anywhere, anytime, for as long as you need to. If you're in the car, pull over and park. Try to lead the pain instead of letting the pain lead you.
- Practice self-kindness every day. You deserve it.
- Draw upon your religious or spiritual beliefs.
- Make an anniversary reaction plan.
- Prepare answers to the question: "How are you?"
- Try the "stay busy" approach and find a balance between being too busy (avoidance) and being busy enough to give your mind a short break from grief.
- Read grief books and articles by grief experts.

Social

- Check your support system. Do you have people of different ages and skills? If not, add new names and contact info to your system.
- Find comfort in friends. One friend can lead you through the darkness.
- Laughter is good medicine. Laugh whenever you can.
- If you hear a tactless comment, diffuse the hurt by seeing the caring behind the comment.

- Help others when you feel stronger. Call them on the phone, email them, grocery shop for them, invite them to lunch, or give them this book.

Family

- Fix a dinner that includes your loved one's favorite foods.
- Make a memory cookbook. Give copies to other family members.
- Learn more about your family history. You may wish to sign up for a genealogy test with a company that specializes in this.
- Keep some family traditions from a previous generation.
- Create new traditions for your family.
- Set a few goals and work to achieve them.
- Live the values that have been important to your family and pass them on to the next generation.

Recreational

- Read for pleasure.
- Watch relaxing television programs.
- Make quiet time part of each day.
- Let nature comfort you. Get a bird feeder and keep track of the birds you see. Photograph the same tree during different seasons. Plant a container garden and care for it.
- Reward yourself after a positive day.
- Buy a new T-shirt.
- Get a new library card.
- Take a painting class.
- Indulge in chocolate or another treat you love.

In the space below, feel free to list your own self-care ideas.
Your ideas could help a grieving family member, friend, neighbor, or stranger.

Words of Hope

Tomorrow hopes we have learned something from yesterday.
— **John Wayne**

Expressing grief in words is a journey of its own. Along the way, you learn about the kindness of others and the resilience of the human spirit. You also discover new things about yourself. If your grief journey is anything like mine, writing will guide you toward hope and, in time, a new life. Writing really does help you heal.

The more you write, the more you learn.

Every time I finish writing a book, I think it's my last. When my husband was alive, he was amused by this idea. He knew I would keep writing. "While you're up, write me a book," he often joked. Sometimes it took months to identify the topic of my next book, but I did it. I continued to write through tragedy, illness, and anniversary reactions.

Volkan and Zintl write about the human spirit. They say some people manage grief effectively and others don't. What's the difference? "The right developmental push—the death of a child, a new and fulfilling love, a wise therapist—is sometimes all that is needed to help us discover the resources to manage conflict and overcome the likely complication of mourning."[46]

Writing was my developmental push and could be yours. I recognized this push when my sense of humor returned. With each passing month, the spark of humor became brighter, and I saw laughter as a sign of recovery. While I'm amazed by my recovery, I know it came from self-examination, grief work, persistence, and my wacky sense of humor. Life feels good, I'm happy, and I'm writing full steam ahead.

You may not be in full-steam-ahead mode yet. Still, writing about your grief journey is a brain exercise, one that helps you track feelings, retrieve pictures and words from memory, and add new words to your vocabulary.

Words tell who you are, where you came from, what you are facing, how you are coping, and where you are headed. The words you choose reveal your struggle to survive. Words are powerful. Let writing empower you.

Harold S. Kushner wrote *When Bad Things Happen to Good People* because his fourteen-year-old son Aaron died: "I wanted to write a book that could be given to a person who has been hurt by life—by death, by illness or injury, by rejection and disappointment—and who knows in his heart that if there is justice in the world, he deserved better."[47]

Rabbi Kushner's book became a bestseller. He helped members of his temple, people of other faiths, people who doubted God, people who believed, and people who felt lost. Writing changed Kushner's life and could change yours. Though you may not write a bestseller, write from your heart and soul. Feelings can become clearer when you read printed words on a page. The words you write help you find and walk your healing path.

Grief is transforming. After writing in this book, you may write your own book for peace of

---

46 Volkan and Zintl, *Life After Loss*, 60.
47 Kushner, *When Bad Things Happen*, 7.

mind, for the family, or for others. You've come to the end of this book. Writer and reader may part ways here, but we will always be joined together by grief. I send you virtual hugs and sincere wishes for a good life, one filled with love, laughter, and newfound joy.

CONCLUSION

A Good Ending to a Grief Story

I wake up every morning with a great desire to live joyfully.
— **Anna Howard Shaw**

Many people have asked what happened to the twins, my husband, and me. John and I were GRGs—grandparents raising grandchildren—for seven years. Not all GRGs have good endings to their stories. We did, and the ending is inspiring, encouraging, and miraculous—an ending worthy of a Hollywood movie.

Both twins graduated from high school with honors, and we helped them with their college searches. Yes, I was lonely when the twins went to college, but it was a good kind of loneliness. The twins were following their mother's wishes and making the most of their education.

My granddaughter attended Coe College in Cedar Rapids, Iowa, and graduated Magna Cum Laude. My grandson attended the University of Minnesota in Minneapolis and graduated Summa Cum Laude. He is also a graduate of the Mayo Clinic Alix School of Medicine, where he is now a radiology resident. To my surprise, I am now a great-grandmother. My granddaughter married a minister, and they are parents of two toddler boys. She is also a talented independent photographer. Because I live in Minnesota and her family lives in Michigan, I don't see my great-grandchildren often. When I do see them, the time we spend together is extra special.

The twins were living with us when John's aorta dissected. He had emergency surgery, and though he survived, he was paraplegic and in a wheelchair for the rest of his life. John couldn't live in a three-story house, so I built a one-level townhome for us, and we lived there for five years. When we were there, I was diagnosed with endometrial cancer and had successful surgery for it. Later, I was diagnosed with acute heart failure, had open heart surgery, and now have a pig valve in my heart.

John continued to get weaker. The time had come to move to a retirement community with supportive services. We moved to Charter House, which is owned and operated by Mayo Clinic. He lived in our apartment for a year and died of advanced prostate cancer, heart disease, and other complications. Caring for John was a sacred experience. As his health failed, my stress level and blood pressure ramped up.

To cope with stress, I would doodle for fifteen to twenty minutes every morning. After doodling, I felt relaxed and ready to return to caregiving. Doodle art eventually led me to create a book about doodling to heal from grief, which paved the way for my second career as a doodle artist. I converted John's bedroom, which had become a place of sadness, into my art studio, now a place of joy. The room is a riot of color, and every wall is covered with doodle art.

"Your art makes me happy," is the comment I hear most often, and that makes me happy too.

Shortly after John died, *Grief Doodling: Bringing Back Your Smiles* was published, and it won several awards. I continued to write about grief and speak about it via Zoom and at national and local conferences. I still believe writing your grief story helps you heal. Indeed, my belief is stronger than ever, and the benefits are many: creativity, insight, discovery, knowledge, solutions, strength, self-worth, self-care, and faith in the future.

Writing about grief often leads me to ideas for books. These ideas come to me at odd times: when I'm in the car, at the grocery store, or waiting for a doctor's appointment. I keep a small pad in my purse to jot down ideas. One of these ideas inspired a leadership book for young children called *Ready, Set, Lead!*, which I co-wrote with a friend who has a leadership business. At eighty-seven years of age, writing keeps my mind sharp.

Writing also helps me to understand life, and that's one of the reasons I wrote *Grief in Your Words*. I hope this book helps you navigate your grief journey. More importantly, I hope it helps you discover new things about yourself. Writing can help you create a new life, the one you seek and deserve. You are a story in action.

Tell it.

Other Journal Ideas to Explore

Margaret Atwood says, "A word after a word is power." Think about that for a minute. Where does the power of words come from? It comes from thinking, honesty, persistence, and courage. It takes courage to keep going. Even when you don't feel like it, you write a few words about how you're feeling.

Reading and responding to *Grief in Your Words* are acts of courage. You have countless words inside you, power to be unleashed and used constructively. What could you write about? Here are some suggestions. You may have more ideas of your own.

- Describe your loved one's personality.
- What do you miss most about your loved one?
- Write about your hobbies and other things you like to do.
- Write about the times you said "no thank you" in self-preservation.
- Write about the times you gladly said "yes" and had a good time.
- Give yourself a boost and write about your best qualities.
- Brainstorm about your dreams for the future.
- Write about the ways you've helped yourself.
- Consider the steps you need to take to get to the future you envision.
- Detail your loved one's main strength and how it helps you now.
- Write a letter to your loved one and keep it for future reference.
- Think of ways to memorialize your loved one. Take action on one idea.

Journal

Support for You

Note: Website addresses and phone numbers are subject to change. For additional support, contact the local Department of Social Services or your faith community.

AARP: American Association of Retired Persons: Offers articles and tips on final days, planning a memorial service, after-death checklist, a new normal, and other topics.
  Website: https://www.aarp.org/caregiving/grief-loss-end-of-life
  Phone: (888) 687-2277

American Psychological Association: Offers resources and webinars on various grief-related topics.
  Website: https://www.apa.org
  Phone: (202) 336-5500

Association for Death Education and Counseling: International organization for those working in the field of bereavement counseling. Offers fellowship training in thanatology (scientific study of death, grief, loss) and a yearly conference.
  Website: www.adec.org
  Phone: (612) 337-1808

Bereaved Parents of the USA: A nonprofit organization that includes local chapters, an online newsletter, and an annual conference.

Website: https://www.bereavedparentsusa.org

Phone: (845) 489-6373

Center for Grief Recovery and Therapeutic Services: For individuals, couples, partnerships, corporations, and organizations. Empowers people to heal their own lives, offers grief counseling.

Website: https://www.griefcounselor.org

Phone: (773) 274-4600

The Compassionate Friends: A nonprofit organization for parents, siblings, and grandparents who suffered the loss of a child. Includes over six hundred local chapters and a yearly conference.

Website: http://compassionatefriends.org

Phone: (877) 969-0010

Elisabeth Kübler-Ross Foundation: Grief education on a variety of topics, grief support, and palliative care education.

Website: https://www.ekrfoundation.org

Phone: (602) 319-2974

First Hour Grief Response: Mentoring, art therapy program, suicide prevention, and resiliency program for students.

Website: https://www.firsthourgrief.org

Phone: (502) 791-9938

Grief in Common: Offers many kinds of support, including creating a profile to connect with others, sharing stories, study, coaching, and live chat feature.

    Website: https://www.griefincommon.com

    Phone: (424) 265-1818

GriefNet: Online support community for all types of loss, uses a multidimensional approach to life.

    Website: https://rivendell.org/

GriefShare: Based on biblical principles, provides support groups in US, Canada, and forty other countries; charges \$15–\$26 fee for registration and refreshments.

Website: www.griefshare.org

    Phone: (800) 395-5755, US and Canada

    (919) 562-2112, International

The Grief Toolbox: A resource that includes articles and products about grief healing and renewal.

    Website: https://thegrieftoolbox.com

    Phone: (603) 791-0999

HEARTBEAT: A nonprofit, international organization for survivors of suicide; offers support groups and resources.

    Website: https://www.heartbeatsurvivorsaftersuicide.org

    Phone: (888) 481-2448

Hospice Foundation of America: Provides leadership training in hospice, philosophy of care, and resources.

    Website: https://hospicefoundation.org

    Phone: (202) 457-5811

My Grief Angels: A website with a chat feature; focuses on workplace grief and pet loss.

    Website: https://www.mygriefangels.org

    Phone: (936) 217-3205

Open to Hope: A nonprofit foundation that has online support, radio, podcasts, television, webinars, books, and a free International Day of Healing online conference.

    Website: www.opentohope.com

    Phone: Not available

Bibliography

Adams, Kathleen. *Journal to the Self: Twenty-Two Paths to Personal Growth.* (New York: Grand Central Publishing. 2009.)

Adams, Kathleen. "Managing Grief through Journal Writing." Journal Therapy. Accessed August 9, 2023. https://journaltherapy.com/wp-content/uploads/2015/04/Article-KA-Managing-Grief-through-Journal-Writing.pdf.

"Anniversary Reactions to a Traumatic Event: The Recovery Continues." MentalHelp.net. Accessed May 25, 2023. https://www.mentalhelp.net/ptsd/anniversary-reactions-to-a-traumatic-event. Baldwin, Christina. *One to One: Self-Understanding Through Journal Writing.* (Maryland: M. Evans & Company. 1991.)

Bernstein, Judith R. *When the Bough Breaks: Forever After the Death of a Son or Daughter.* (Kansas City: Andrews McMeel Publishing. 1998.)

Deits, Bob. *Life After Loss: A Practical Guide to Renewing Your Life After Experiencing Major Loss.* (New York: Hachette Books. 2017.)

Goleman, Daniel. *Emotional Intelligence: Why It Can Matter More Than IQ.* (New York: Random House. 2012.)

Kessler, David. *Finding Meaning: The Sixth Stage of Grief.* (New York: Scribner. 2019.)

Kottler, Jeffrey A. *The Language of Tears.* (New York: John Wiley & Sons. 1996.)

Kushner, Harold S. *When Bad Things Happen to Good People.* (New York: Knopf Doubleday Publishing, 2004.)

Oates, Joyce Carol and Meghan O'Rourke. "Why We Write About Grief." *New York Times.* February 26, 2011. https://www.nytimes.com/2011/02/27/weekinreview/27grief.html.

Oliver, Mary. *Thirst.* (Boston: Beacon Press. 2006.)

Rando, Therese A. *How to Go On Living When Someone You Love Dies.* (New York: Random House. 1991.)

Reid, Ruthanne. "Show, Don't Tell: How to Write the Stages of Grief." The Write Practice. Accessed August 9, 2023. https://thewritepractice.com/writing-grief.

Seal, Moorea. *52 Lists for Happiness: Weekly Journaling, Inspiration for Positivity, Balance, and Joy.* (Seattle: Sasquatch Books. 2016.)

Stang, Heather. "9 Self-Care Tips for Grief: Reduce Your Suffering in Mind, Body & Spirit." Mindfulness and Grief. September 13, 2021. https://mindfulnessandgrief. com/9-self-care-tips-for-grief.

"Stress Relief from Laughter? It's No Joke." Mayo Clinic. July 29, 2021. https://www.mayoclinic. org/healthy-lifestyle/stress-management/in-depth/stress-relief/art-20044456.

Tatelbaum, Judy. *The Courage to Grieve: The Classic Guide to Creative Living, Recovery, and Growth Through Grief.* (New York: HarperCollins. 2009.)

Veninga, Robert L. *A Gift of Hope: How We Survive Our Tragedies.* (New York: Random House. 1996.)

Viorst, Judith. *Necessary Losses: The Loves, Illusions, Dependencies, and Impossible Expectations that All of Us Have to Give Up in Order to Grow.* (New York: Simon & Schuster. 2010.)

Volkan, Vamik D. and Elizabeth Zintl. *Life After Loss: The Lessons of Grief.* (New York: Taylor & Francis. 2018.)

"Worden's Four Tasks of Mourning," Our House Grief Support Center. Accessed June 11, 2023. https://www.ourhouse-grief.org/grief-pages/grieving-adults/four-tasks-of-mourning.

Ziccarello, Roe. "10 Steps to Heal Your Grief." Trans4mind. Accessed April 27, 2023. https://trans4mind.com/counterpoint/index-emotional-intelligence/ziccarello.html.

More Grief Healing Books
by Harriet Hodgson

Winning: A Story of Grief and Renewal

Daisy a Day: Hope for a Grieving Heart

Grief Doodling: Bringing Back Your Smiles (author and illustrator)

From Sad to Glad: A Workbook for Grieving Kids (ages 4–7)

From Darkness to Sunshine: A Workbook for Grieving Kids (ages 8–12)

Writing to Recover Journal

Happy Again: Your New and Meaningful Life After Loss

101 Affirmations to Ease Your Grief Journey: Words of Comfort, Words of Hope

Seed Time: Growing from Life's Disappointments, Losses, and Sorrows

Smiling Through Your Tears: Anticipating Grief, coauthor Lois Krahn, MD.

About the Author

Photo by Haley Earley

Harriet Hodgson has been a freelancer for forty-eight years and is the author of thousands of articles and forty-six books. She has a BS in Early Childhood Education from Wheelock College of Education and Human Development at Boston University, an MA in Art Education from the University of Minnesota, and additional graduate training. Hodgson is also a certified art therapy coach.

She is a member of the Association of Health Care Journalists, Alliance of Independent Authors, and Minnesota Coalition for Death Education and Support.

Hodgson's grief writing comes from her extensive experience as a bereaved mother, daughter, sister, daughter-in-law, mother-in-law, cousin, and friend.

A popular speaker, Hodgson has appeared on more than 190 talk shows, dozens of BlogTalkRadio shows and television stations, including CNN. She has given presentations at public health, Alzheimer's, caregiving, and bereavement conferences. Hodgson also gives Zoom workshops about grief and reducing stress with doodle art.

The award-winning author lives in Rochester, Minnesota. For more information about this grandmother, great-grandmother, community volunteer, speaker, and doodle artist, please visit www.harriethodgson.net.